W9-CMS-712

KENKA BANCHO Otome

2

LOVE'S BATTLE ROYALE

STORY & ART BY
CHIE SHIMADA

Original concept by Spike Chunsoft
Video game developed by Red Entertainment

KENKA BANCHO Otome

LOVE'S BATTLE ROYALE

2

CONTENTS

CHAPTER 5 4

CHAPTER 6 49

CHAPTER 7 91

CHAPTER 8 141

ACT LIKE A BEST FRIEND

I WANT TO RECORD EVERYTHING ABOUT YOU

KENKA BANCHO
Otome
LOVE'S BATTLE ROYALE
Chapter
5
10
LET'S PLAY A GAME

I'M ALWAYS WATCHING OVER YOU

WASH BLOOD WITH BLOOD

獅窩學
THE INFAMOUS ALL-BOYS SCHOOL FOR DELINQUENTS...
...SHISHIKU ACADEMY.
FIGHTS AND BRAWLS ARE NOTHING NEW.
BEING POWERFUL IS ALL THAT COUNTS IN THIS SAVAGE WORLD.
*Flag: Shishiku Academy
TMP
HEY, THAT GUY IN THE MIDDLE MUST BE...
SHH!
AVOID EYE CONTACT. HE'LL KILL YOU.
HE BEAT KIRA, WHO'S A SECOND-YEAR.
THEN HE'S THE MOST DANGEROUS, HUH.

HIS TWO HENCHMEN ARE WITH HIM...
HE MUST BE UP TO SOMETHING.
I, HIKARU ONIGASHIMA, HAVE FINALLY BECOME...
...THE BOSS OF THE SECOND-YEARS!
HEY, GUYS.
GASP
THOSE GUYS AREN'T MY HENCHMEN.
THEY'RE MY-
YEEK!
DASH
FORGIVE US!
?!
HUH?
I HAVEN'T DONE ANYTHING...
YAARGH
TMP TMP TMP
POFF
DON'T STRESS ABOUT IT, HIKARU.

FIRST-YEAR
TOTOMARU MINOWA
ON TOP OF IT...
...YOU'RE AN ONIGASHIMA.
THE ONIGASHIMA ARE A YAKUZA FAMILY...
...AND I, HIKARU, AM THEIR SON.
THAT'S RIGHT.
YOU GUYS...
NO OTHER FIRST- OR SECOND-YEARS CAN BEAT YOU...
...OF COURSE THEY'RE SCARED OF YOU.
FIRST-YEAR
TAKAYUKI KONPARU
I'VE WORKED HARD TO ACHIEVE THAT GOAL.
THE SONS MUST BECOME THE BOSS OF SHISHIKU.
THE ONIGASHIMA FAMILY HAS A RULE.
BUT...
Ha ha!
DON'T BE SO GLUM!
AND NOW I'M BEING AVOIDED HERE...
TEARY
BUT BECAUSE I'M STRONG AT FIGHTING, EVERYONE STAYED AWAY FROM ME IN THE PAST.

WE'RE HERE FOR YOU.
AT THIS SCHOOL...
...I MADE MY VERY FIRST FRIENDS.
YES!
FOCUS INSTEAD ON HOW TO BECOME BOSS OF THE THIRD-YEARS...
IT'S DANGEROUS WITHOUT A GOOD PLAN.
OH... YOU'RE RIGHT.
BUT THERE'S SO MUCH BLOOD!
IT HAPPENS ALL THE TIME.
LEAVE HIM ALONE, HIKARU.
SPLURK
URGH!
PLUB PLUB PLUB
I-I'M OKAY...
TOTO-MARU?!

THANKS FOR THINKING OF ME...
...KONPARU.
...
I HAVEN'T DONE ANYTHING...
HE'S RIGHT.
YOU NEED A GOOD PLAN.
GACK
POKE POKE POKE
EEK!!
OTHER-WISE YOU MIGHT GET ATTACKED LIKE THIS. ♡

M... MIRAKO!
NOT AGAIN!
You jerk!
STOP GIVING HIKARU A HARD TIME EVERY TIME YOU SEE HIM!
WELL, WELL... ARE YOU JEALOUS, KIDDO?
WHAT'RE YOU TALKING ABOUT?!
I UNDERSTAND. HIKARU IS SUCH A CUTIE PIE...
HA HA! THAT WAS QUITE A SCREAM.
SECOND-YEAR YUTA MIRAKO
HE COULD EASILY BE A GIRL.
GULP
BAMP
Ow.
MIRAKO.
DON'T GIVE THE YOUNGER STUDENTS A HARD TIME.
OH...
SECOND-YEAR RINTARO KIRA

KIRA!
BEATING THE THIRD-YEARS WILL BE DIFFICULT.
HIKARU.
GULP
STAY FOCUSED.
SINCE I STARTED AT SHISHIKU...
...LOTS OF THINGS HAVE HAPPENED.
I DON'T ENJOY FIGHTING, BUT...
I WILL!

Dang.
RINTARO ALWAYS SAYS...
...THE BEST LINES.
FOR ALL MY FRIENDS WHO SUPPORT ME...
...I WANT TO DO MY BEST AS "HIKARU ONIGASHIMA."
WHAT?
WHY DO I SAY IT LIKE THAT?
IT'S BECAUSE ...
YOU'RE HOME, HINAKO!
TUP TUP TUP
SWEET
THANKS FOR PRETENDING TO BE ME AGAIN. ♡
HERE IS...
...THE REAL HIKARU.

HIKARU, YOU DON'T HAVE TO DRESS LIKE A GIRL AT HOME.
TEE HEE
YOU CAN NEVER LET YOUR GUARD DOWN, RIGHT?
YOU KNOW I'M NOT LIKE THAT.
YOUNG BOSS, YOU LOOK BEAUTIFUL IN EVERY-THING!
LOOK THIS WAY PLEASE!
I GUESS ...
KLIK
KLIK
I THOUGHT I WAS AN ORPHAN...
...BUT SOMEONE APPEARED IN FRONT OF ME AT THE ENTRANCE CEREMONY FOR THE GIRLS' SCHOOL.
HE CLAIMED HE WAS MY LONG-LOST TWIN BROTHER.
HUH?
HE HATES FIGHTING, AND BECAUSE I'M GOOD AT IT, HE PROPOSED WE SWITCH PLACES.
HE SORT OF THREAT-ENED ME...
...AND NOW HERE WE ARE TODAY.
HERE, THIS IS FOR YOU.
!
IT'S A GIFT I PICKED UP FOR YOU WHEN I WENT SHOPPING WITH MOMO.
WAGGLE
I COULDN'T DECIDE BETWEEN THE TWO COLORS...
THIS...
...IS MY FAVORITE CHARACTER!

THANK YOU, HIKARU.
I'LL TREASURE IT FOR THE REST OF MY LIFE!
GLOW
Hmph. IT'S NO BIG DEAL.
WE SEEM TO HAVE MORE OF A BROTHER-AND-SISTER RELATIONSHIP NOW.
IT MAKES ME HAPPY.
I'll put it on my phone.
I WANT TO BECOME THE BOSS...

Volume 2! Yay!

Hello, I'm Shimada. Thank you very much for picking up volume 2!! ✧✧

So much is going on! I got word that *Kenka Bancho Otome* will become an anime. But it'll make me really happy if you continue to enjoy this manga version as well.

The next sidebar will be about my visit to the fifth recording of "Tokoton Totokon Radio" featuring Totomaru (played by KENN) and Konparu (played by Shouta Aoi).

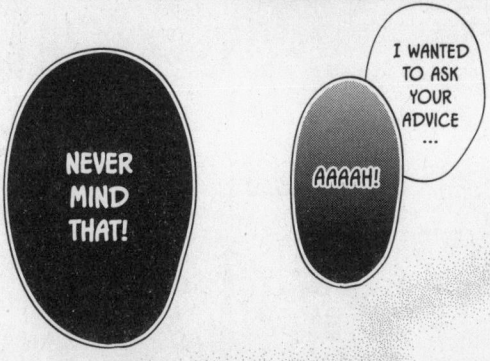

HUH?
HINAKO.
B-BUT...
IT'S ENOUGH THAT YOU BEAT THE FIRST-YEARS AND THE SECOND-YEARS SO QUICKLY.
YOU CAN WAIT UNTIL YOU'RE A SECOND-YEAR TO BATTLE AGAIN.
STOP TRYING TO BECOME THE BOSS FOR NOW.
YOUNG BOSS...
OH
SAKAGUCHI MIGHT KNOW.
WHY THE SUDDEN CHANGE OF HEART?
HE WAS SO INSISTENT UNTIL NOW.
BEEP
GRAB

HERE WE GO! ALL ABOUT TOKO RADIO!!

KENN, who plays Totomaru, is easy-going and playful—just like his character.

Shouta Aoi is the complete opposite to his cool characterization of Konparu. He's cute and quite feminine. (?!)

This is what they call each other, and the conversation was easy, but...
Someone finally makes a guest appearance in the fifth episode.

GURK GURK GURK GURK GURK

SA-KA-GU-CHI! ♡

MAKE DINNER! ♡

GURK

Y-YES SIR!

DON'T READ TOO MUCH INTO WHAT I SAID.

I'M JUST LOOKING OUT FOR YOU AS YOUR BIG BROTHER.

TAKE IT EASY FOR A WHILE...

...HINAKO. ♡

DONG

DONG

STILL...

HEY, TOTOMARU, KEEP A LOW PROFILE.
THEY'RE REALLY INTO THIS.
MRMR
THE ATMOSPHERE HERE IS REALLY DIFFERENT.
THE CLASS-ROOMS FOR THE THIRD-YEARS.
MRMR
JOLT
YOU'RE NOT THIRD-YEARS, ARE YOU?
HEY, YOU GUYS...
I THINK WE SHOULD JUST GO FOR IT.
WE CAME THIS FAR.
COME ON, STAND UP STRAIGHT!
CRAP! WHEN WAS THE LAST TIME HE CAME BY?!
THIS IS MY FIRST TIME SEEING HIM.
HOUOU IS COMING!
Huh?
YOU'RE THAT FIRST-YEAR!
WE GOT BUSTED RIGHT AWAY.
Wait!
OH, UM...
DASH
GET OUT OF THE WAY, PUNKS!

WICKED!
THE LEGENDARY BOSS.
WHAT?
WHEN HE WAS IN YEAR ONE...
...HE BEAT EVERYONE AT SHISHIKU WITHIN ONE MONTH.
WHO?
WHISH
HOUOU ONIGASHIMA!

ONIGA-SHIMA...
WHAT?
YO.
IT'S REALLY YOU, HIKARU.
IT'S BEEN A WHILE.

HEY, FIRST-YEARS. HOW'S IT GOING?
I'M HIKARU'S OLDER BROTHER.
WELL...
...WE DO HAVE DIFFERENT MOMS.
!
HIKARU ...
WHO'S THIS?!
WHAT'S GOING ON?!
HIKARU NEVER TOLD ME THERE WERE OTHER ONIGASHIMA FAMILY MEMBERS.
IT CAN'T BE.
HIKARU ISN'T MY ONLY SIBLING...
I HAVE ANOTHER OLDER BROTHER?!
STEP BACK, BOTH OF YOU.
SWIP
HEY.
WE NEVER KNEW YOU HAD AN OLDER BROTHER.

EVEN IF YOU'RE...
...MY OLDER BROTHER...
I...
I'M GOING TO BE THE STRONGEST AT THIS SCHOOL!
THAT'S WHAT I PROMISED HIKARU.
SMILE
HE'S COMING AT ME!
JOLT
HIKARU.
WSH

MUSS
HUH?
MUSS
MUSS
MUSS
MUSS
W...
WAIT!
WHAT?!
B-BROTHER.
YOU CALLED ME BROTHER...
GRIN
YES!
I'M YOUR BIG BROTHER!

SPIN
SPIN
WHAT IS GOING ON?
YOU HAVEN'T GROWN AT ALL.
HOW MANY YEARS HAS IT BEEN?
UP
?!
HE...
...DOESN'T ACT HOSTILE AT ALL.
You're so light, Hikaru!
A smile that melts your heart...
MAYBE THE REA-SON...
OH
FEH
SHOOT! IT'S THE BELL!
DONG DONG
...IS BECAUSE HE DIDN'T WANT ME TO FIGHT HOUOU?
...HIKARU SAID HE WANTED ME TO STOP...

DASH
WE GOTTA GET BACK, HIKARU!
OH!
YOU KNOW...
...YOUR BROTHER SEEMED REALLY HAPPY.
?
MY...
...BIG BROTHER ...
SKWEEZ
IT'S GO GREAT.
I THOUGHT I WOULD BE ALONE FOREVER.
I WAS SURPRISED WHEN I MET HIKARU...
...AND NOW I KNOW I HAVE ANOTHER BROTHER!

IT'S AMAZ-ING.
I'M HOME, HIKARU!
HI...
You rarely text me.
WHAT'S UP? YOU SAID YOU WANTED TO TELL ME SOME-THING?
DID SOMETHING GOOD HAPPEN TODAY?
I HAVE SOME-THING TO TELL YOU TOO-
MY BIG BROTHER.
I MET MY BIG BROTHER HOUOU TODAY.
WHAT ...?
I WAS SO SUR-PRISED...
WHY DIDN'T YOU TELL ME ABOUT HIM?
HOUOU IS REALLY NICE.

HIKARU?
WHY...
...DID YOU SEE HIM WITHOUT TELLING ME?!
JOLT
HUH?
WELL, UM...
YOUNG BOSS, YOUNG MISTRESS, IS SOMETHING WRONG?
Ah.
IT'S ALL RIGHT. WE'RE NOT FIGHTING.
HOUOU AND I JUST CHATTED.
THAT'S NOT IT!
I HATE HIM AND THE ENTIRE ONIGASHIMA FAMILY!
I DON'T EVEN WANT TO HEAR YOU TALK ABOUT HIM!

HIKA–
I'VE NEVER THOUGHT OF THOSE GUYS...
...AS FAMILY.
IF YOU THINK WE'RE ALL THE SAME...
...I'D RATHER BE WITHOUT FAMILY!
YANK
CUT IT...
...OUT.
GRIP
...
HEY...

!
PLEASE STOP, YOUNG MISTRESS!
YOUNG BOSS!
YOUNG MISTRESS DOESN'T KNOW ANYTHING. DON'T TAKE IT OUT ON HER.
BUT...
...SAKAGUCHI...
IT'S HINAKO'S FAULT FOR NOT LISTENING TO ME.
WHY DOES HE...
...SAY THAT?
S...
STUPID HIKARU!

YOUNG MISTRESS!
Please... Don't go...!
HUFF...
HUFF...
FSSH
...
HUFF
HUFF
FSSH
...

FSSSH

AAH...
GRAB
YOU'LL CATCH COLD...
COME WITH ME.
HUH?
WHERE?
MY HOUSE.
THE ONIGASHIMA HOUSE?
OH! UM!! I CAN'T...
I...
FSSH

WHERE ARE WE?
THIS IS WHERE I LIVE.
Come on in.
THE DOOR LOCKS AUTOMATICALLY.
A STUDIO...
LIKE HIKARU...
...HE DOESN'T LIVE AT HOME.
WHY...?
SHFF
SHFF
SHMP
HURRY UP AND CHANGE.
THANKS SO MUCH-
FWUP
HUH?!

HM?
FMP
WHAT'S WRONG?
NOTH-ING.
UM...
I'LL CHANGE IN THERE...
...
GHAK
SLUMP
THAT WAS SHOCKING.
THMP
WE'RE SIBLINGS...
...BUT I JUST REALIZED I'M IN A MAN'S APARTMENT.
THMP THMP
You changed
Just a sec!
GULP
PANIC PANIC

WHAM BAM
OUCH!
OW...
EAT MORE MEAT!
YOU'RE SKIN AND BONES!
HA... HA HA
THOSE ARE WAY TOO BIG FOR YOU.
TOMP
HERE.
HUH?
Hee hee...
HERE'S A CUSHION.
COME CLOSER. IT'S WARMER HERE...
DING
MILK?
DO YOU WANT SUGAR...?
I'M SORRY.
IT'S JUST THAT YOU DON'T SIT STILL...
I FINALLY GOT A SMILE OUT OF YOU.

I'M GLAD.
HIKARU IS SO LUCKY.
HE HAS SOMEONE TO CHEER HIM UP.
IS IT BECAUSE I'M...
...YOUR LITTLE BROTHER?
WHY ARE YOU SO NICE TO ME...?
HUH?

...WAS ALWAYS ALONE.
...
SO LUCKY.
DON'T TALK LIKE THAT!
I'D RATHER BE WITHOUT FAMILY.
...AS FAMILY.
I'VE NEVER THOUGHT OF THOSE GUYS...
HOUOU DOESN'T KNOW THAT I EXIST...
I WAS...
...TOSSED OUT BY THE SAME ONIGASHIMA FAMILY YOU DIDN'T WANT TO BE A PART OF.
I CAN'T STAND THIS...
...EVEN THOUGH I'M HIS LITTLE SISTER.
...ANYMORE.
IT'S AS IF I DON'T MATTER AT ALL.

POFF
POFF
Ow!
Ouch.
DON'T UNDER-ESTIMATE ME.
SUFF
HIKARU...
...I WOULD HAVE HELPED YOU REGARDLESS OF WHO YOU ARE.
HELPING THOSE IN TROUBLE...
...IS WHAT BEING A MAN IS ALL ABOUT.
HOUO-

BY THE WAY...
...THE OTHER DAY, YOU CALLED ME BROTHER FOR THE FIRST TIME.
YOU USED TO REFUSE TO EVEN LOOK AT ME BEFORE.
IS THAT RIGHT ?!
SHOOT! I'M CONTRA-DICTING HIKARU.
I'M HAPPY.
I FEEL LIKE WE'RE FINALLY GETTING CLOSER.
BMP
IF YOU DON'T MIND...
JUST ONE MORE TIME...
...WOULD YOU CALL ME BROTHER?
YEAH...
I'M ALSO...

...HAPPY.
...THIS IS...
...MEANS...
THAT HE'S HAPPY I CALLED HIM BROTHER...
...A PRECIOUS MEMORY HOUOU AND I SHARE.
WE HAD NOTHING BEFORE.
I KNOW.
?! HIKA-
SURE...
...BIG BROTHER.

THANKS A LOT.
NO PROBLEM. STAY SAFE.
GNAK
OKAY, WHAT AM I GOING TO DO NOW?
SPLASH
THIS IS THE BEGINNING...
...OF SHARING MANY MEMORIES TOGETHER.

HE MIGHT CUT TIES WITH ME.
HIKARU MUST BE REALLY ANGRY.
IT'S THE FIRST TIME I TALKED BACK TO HIM.
HUFF
HUFF
HUFF
HINAKO!
EVEN SO...
...HIKARU AND I WILL CONTINUE TO...
...MAKE...
...MEMORIES...
OH?!
HIKARU?!
IT'S NOT LIKE YOU.
WHAT HAPPENED? YOU'RE A MESS...
Where's your wig?

GURK!!
HE'S REALLY ANGRY.
AT LEAST TAKE YOUR PHONE WITH YOU! WERE YOU BORN YESTERDAY?!
YOU JUST TOOK OFF...!!
WAIT...
HIKA-
YARL
YARL
YARL
IT'S ALL YOUR FAULT, HINAKO!
YOU KNOW EXACTLY WHAT'S WRONG!
OH...
YOU HAVE THE SAME STRAP...
I WAS SO...
I TRIED CALLING YOU SO MANY TIMES...
I...

ARE YOU EVEN LISTENING TO ME?!
NEVER MIND! I'M SORRY!
RAWR
AND... UM...
MAYBE HIKARU...
...HAS HIS REASONS TOO.
I'M SORRY.
...
...
ME TOO...
POFF
POFF
TUG
!

IT DOESN'T MATTER NOW.
I FORGIVE YOU.
AFTER ALL...
...I'M YOUR BIG BROTHER.
SAY...
HIKARU...

LET'S GO, HINAKO.
OKAY.
YOUNG BOSS! YOUNG MISTRESS ...!
I'M SO GLAD YOU'RE SAFE!
IT'S STRANGE.
THAT HUG.
IF I TOLD YOU IT'S THE SAME AS HOUOU'S...
...WOULD YOU GET MAD AT ME AGAIN?
AT SCHOOL...
...I FIGHT ALL THE TIME.
BUT THIS WAS THE FIRST TIME...
...I FOUGHT WITH MY BROTHER.
Sakaguchi! I want to go to the hot spring!
Yes sir!! I'll bring the car over right now!!

Chapter
6

BLUE SKY.
SPAR-KLING OCEAN.
I'M ABOUT TO EXPERIENCE SOMETHING NEW.
VROOM
WOW...!

MY NAME IS HIKARU ONIGASHIMA.
I MAY NOT LOOK LIKE IT...
...BUT I'M A STUDENT AT THE INFAMOUS ALL-BOYS SCHOOL FOR DELIQUENTS...
...SHISHIKU ACADEMY.
Tee hee!
THE SEA ISN'T GOING ANYWHERE.
WHOA, WHOA...
...!
H-HURRY...!
EAGER
EAGER
WHO ARE YOU PRETENDING TO BE, TOTOMARU?
OOPS...
POFF
SORRY.
B-DMP
AND YOU...
IS THAT HOW A TOP BOSS AT SHISHIKU ACTS?
OH, UM...
WHAT?!
AREN'T YOU TAKING YOUR SHIRT OFF, HIKARU?
GOOD THING WE WORE SWIM TRUNKS.
LET'S GO!
I GET SUNBURNS EASILY...
KLENCH
!!
FIP

I CAN NEVER TAKE MY SHIRT OFF...
...BECAUSE...
Phew.
THAT WAS CLOSE...
REALLY? BUMMER.
NOD
NOD
...I'M ACTUALLY A GIRL.
...EVERYONE WILL FIND OUT...
HE LOOKED JUST LIKE ME AND CLAIMED TO BE THE HEIR TO THE ONIGASHIMA YAKUZA FAMILY.
SOMEONE CAME TO ME ON THE DAY OF MY HIGH SCHOOL ENTRANCE CEREMONY.
I, HINAKO NAKAYAMA, GREW UP IN AN ORPHANAGE.
I'm your twin!
I'm Young Boss's minder.
THE ONIGASHIMA FAMILY RULE IS TO "BECOME NUMBER ONE AT SHISHIKU."
BEFORE I KNEW IT, I GOT BAMBOOZLED INTO...
...SWITCHING ROLES WITH HIKARU.
YOU CAN'T SWIM IF YOU CAN'T TAKE YOUR SHIRT OFF.
WANT TO PLAY BEACH VOLLEYBALL INSTEAD?
!

DIDN'T YOU SAY YOU'VE NEVER BEEN TO THE BEACH WITH FRIENDS BEFORE?
IDIOT...
BONK
DON'T WORRY ABOUT ME. GO SWIM-
AH!
THERE'S NO POINT IF WE DON'T HANG OUT TOGETHER!
TOTO-MARU...
KON-PARU...
YOU'RE SO OVER-THE-TOP!
HA HA HA
THIS...
SHK
SHK
THIS'LL BE A ONCE-IN-A-LIFETIME MEMORY!
I NEVER IMAG-INED...
...LIFE COULD BE SO DAZ-ZLING.

?
THESE ARE...
...THE BEST DAYS OF MY LIFE!!
It's hot.
I SHOULD HAVE BROUGHT A STRAW HAT.
HIKARU BURNS EASILY...
SPLASH
HE CAN WALK ALONG THE BEACH...
TOTOMARU...
THIS WAY.
TOTOMARU...

B-BMP
YOUR FACE IS RED.
I HOPE YOU DON'T HAVE HEAT-STROKE.
OH NO... THIS IS...
B-BMP
B-BMP
B-DMP
WHAA!
TOTOMARU?
WHY DO YOU KEEP LOOKING AWAY?
DAMN. WHAT'S WRONG WITH ME? WHY DO I HAVE THESE WEIRD THOUGHTS?
Huh?
No way!
Did you hear?
GLOOM
FORGET ABOUT HIM.
I'M READY, HIKARU.
TOTOMARU REALLY IS JUST LIKE A BOY...
WHAT?
Ready for what?
He is so embar-rassed.
GASP
MAYBE IT'S BETTER IF I DON'T DENY IT?!
N-NO...!!
NOW I GET IT...

MRMR
MRMR
EVERYONE ON THE BEACH IS LOOKING AT US...
LOUDER!
FIVE, SIX, SEVEN, EIGHT...
Five, six, seven...
One, two, three, four...
ONE, TWO, THREE, FOUR...
Bend your body to the side
THE OCEAN IS DANGEROUS, SO ALWAYS BE ON ALERT.
GUARD YOURSELF AGAINST HEATSTROKE TOO.
Ah!
BEEP
IF YOU DON'T WARM UP, YOU'LL GET HURT.
KONPARU IS SO SERIOUS...
THERE.
OH.
...MAKE ME THINK KONPARU IS SUCH A BIG BROTHER...
THINGS LIKE THIS...

The question is, why do you always get a bloody nose?
NEVER MIND THAT.
YOU ALWAYS IGNORE ME WHEN I COLLAPSE WITH A BLOODY NOSE!
IT'S DEFINITELY DIFFERENT!
YUP...! FAVORED TREATMENT AMONG FRIENDS IS A BAD THING!
There, there.
You guys.
GWAR
YOU TOO, TOTO-MARU... I WON'T HELP YOU IF YOU DROWN.
WHY DO I GET DIFFERENT TREATMENT?!
HEY, YOU...!
URGH
COME ON, HIKARU, SAY SOMETHING.
HUH?
DON'T YOU THINK SO, HIKARU?
WHAT?
BAM
YOU'RE IN MY WAY!
AAH!
WHAT AM I SUPPOSED TO SAY AT TIMES LIKE THIS?
UM...
I...
W-WELL...

SHOOM
HIKARU! YOU OKAY?!
WHAT ?!
WATCH IT–
YEE!
YUTA!
HE'S SO HAND-SOME! LOOK THIS WAY!
I found a shell!
THAT'S...
MIRAKO?!
AND ...

KIRA?!
Look at the camera.
Get closer.
I GET THAT MIRAKO IS WORKING...
...BUT WHY ARE THEY HERE?
MIRAKO?! KIRA TOO...
WHO'S THAT OTHER MODEL?
I don't know.
GRAB
SO TRUE.
THEY'RE GORGEOUS.
YO.

YOU...
...SHOVED HIKARU INTO A FACE-PLANT EARLIER.
APOLO-GIZE.
KLENCK
HEY! STOP!
SAY IT PROP-ERLY...
I'LL CALL THE POLICE!
I'M SCARED.
WHO IS THIS GUY?
?!
KONPARU!

IF THIS CONTINUES, KONPARU WILL GET IN TROUBLE BECAUSE OF ME.
I'M NOT HURT OR ANYTHING. DON'T WORRY ABOUT IT.
HIKARU...
THAT'S NOT THE POINT.
HEY, RINTARO, LOOK...
!
YOU TWO! PLEASE BE QUIET!
SHOVE
EEEK!
CAREFUL–
SHIP
SPLASH
HIKARU?!

HIKARU!! I'M–
MY CLOTHES... ...ARE WEIGHING ME DOWN.
BWAH!
MOVE!
GLUP GLUP
!
YHM
SP
YOU OKAY...
...HIKARU?
ASH

Tomoaki Maeno plays Houou Onigashima! Right off the bat...

LET'S GET STRAIGHT TO THE POINT!

The studio came to life with Houou's great lines and wicked conversation skills. It's no wonder he's known as a legendary delinquent...

SPLASH

IT'S SEA-WATER, THAT'S WHY.

SO SALTY...! MY MOUTH...

KOFF...

UHH...

SPLOSH

SPIT IT ALL OUT.

WAIT...

THIS VOICE...

HOUOU...?!

I'M GLAD...
...YOU'RE OKAY.
PHOO
HIKARU!
HEY, FIRST-YEAR PUNKS!
WHY ARE YOU HERE, HOUOU?
I WORK AT THAT BEACHSIDE SNACK BAR.
YAWN
ANY-WAY...
DRY YOURSELF WITH THIS.
GARGLE AND DRINK LOTS OF WATER.
HAVE A SEAT, GUYS.
HOW ABOUT FRIED NOODLES? I'VE GOT SHAVED ICE TOO.
HERE'S SOMETHING SPECIAL FOR YOU, HIKARU.
DILIGENT
DILIGENT

I understand him...
...HE SEEMS LIKE A DOTING BROTHER.
SKFF SKFF SKFF
HA HA HA!
YOU KNOW...
Yo!
YOU GOT A PROBLEM, FIRST-YEAR?
N-NO.
TOTOMARU'S A NICE GUY...
...BIG BROTHER!
H-HIKARU...
AGAIN!
HUH?!
LOOKS LIKE YOU DIDN'T GET HURT. THAT'S GOOD.
Big Brother!
BIG BROTHER
Big Brother!

So what was with that reaction just now?
Aaah.
HIKARU, CHANGE INTO THIS RIGHT NOW.
Ack!
Ow! Ow! Ow!
Huh?
SHAVED ICE
BUT I'M ALMOST DRY...
THAT'S NOT IT.
HELLO.
I TOLD THAT GIRL SHE NEEDS TO BE MORE CAREFUL.
MIRAKO, KIRA!
GEH.
SKINTIGHT
!
YOU DON'T WANT THEM TO FIND OUT, RIGHT?
I SEE. TOUGH LUCK FOR KIRA...
WHAT DO YOU MEAN BY THAT?
THE THEME OF TODAY'S SHOOT WAS MY LIFE OFF THE SET.
I ASKED RINTARO TO COME AS MY FRIEND.
...BUT HOW COME KIRA WAS ALSO AT THE PHOTO SHOOT?
I GET THAT MIRAKO WAS WORKING...
SHAVED ICE
H-HOW EMBARRASSING

HEY, HIKARU...
WHAT DID YOU THINK?
PWOP
EEK.
HA HA
JUST KID-DING.
YOU DID!
HUH?
SMILE
DID I LOOK COOL?
IN EACH SHOT...
...YOU HAD A COMPLETELY DIFFERENT EXPRESSION.
I THINK I NOW KNOW WHY...
...GIRLS GO CRAZY FOR YOU.

SIGH
STOP IT ALREADY...
ARE YOU REALLY A GUY?
MIRAKO ?
WHAT?
DOES HE THINK I'M A GIRL AGAIN?
GRAB
SHUP
HERE'S SOME-THING FOR A SPECIAL FAN. ♡
ACK!
HA HA HA! STOP!
THAT TICKLES...
DEAD SERIOUS ABOUT HIKARU
WHOA...
THAT'S ENOUGH. GET AWAY FROM HIKARU.
HEY.

YARGH
WAAH
Ah ha ha! It's not good for guys to get jealous!
W-what the heck?
KONPARU!
RAMEN
SHAVED ICE
IT SURE WAS.
IT WAS MY FAULT YOU GOT INVOLVED EARLIER–
!
UM...
I'M SORRY.
HIKARU.
THIS IS WHAT I DON'T LIKE ABOUT YOU.

WHAT...?
I'M...
...SORRY.
WHAT DOESN'T HE LIKE ABOUT ME?!
W-WHAT DON'T YOU LIKE?
WHAT AM I GOING TO DO?!
KONPARU IS MAD AT ME.
DON'T YOU GET IT?
IT'S HOW...

VUR
GAAAAH!
?!
LET'S GO, HIKARU! KONPARU!
IT'S AN ALL-OUT WAR NOW!
COME ON.
Ha ha!
?!
TOTO-MARU...
WE WERE IN THE MIDDLE OF–
GACK!
COME ON!
WOOM
WAIT.
WOO! THAT'S KIRA'S KILLER SERVE!!
I HAVE NO INTENTION OF FIGHTING.
TOING
Eek.

WHAT DOESN'T HE LIKE ABOUT ME?
WHAT DID I DO?
WHAT'S HAPPEN-ING?!
SHWAA
SHWAA

In the radio show, the two call each other "Big Brother KENN" and "Shouta," so we wondered what Maeno would want to be called.

You can see the heart symbol after the word!

Is it too cute?

"But we call KENN 'Big Brother,' so will this make him jealous?" asks Aoi, acting like a little devil...!!

KENN and Maeno are the same age, so it's more natural for them to refer to each other without titles.

!!
Sure. Go ahead.
SORRY, ONIGA-SHIMA...
The string broke...
CAN I JUMP IN THE SHOWER FIRST?
SLIP
TMP TMP
I...
I'LL GET THE ICE CREAM!
HIKARU?!
What's with him?
He must really want ice cream.
I WONDER WHAT BOTHERS HIM ABOUT ME.
OK
I DON'T HAVE A CLUE.
SIGH
I KNEW I SHOULDN'T HAVE LOOKED AT THE LOWER PART OF HIS BODY...

THE ICE CREAM WILL MELT.
OH
...HE SAYS HE DOESN'T WANT TO BE MY FRIEND ANYMORE?
KIRA!
I-I'M SORRY... I WAS ZONING OUT.
DID SOME-THING HAPPEN?
BECAUSE HE'S ONE OF MY VERY FIRST FRIENDS...
...I DON'T KNOW WHAT TO DO.
WHAT AM I SUPPOSED TO SAY TO HIM?
WHAT IF...

B-BMP
HUH?
WELL...
I WAS THINKING THIS IS A COINCIDENCE!
I DIDN'T THINK I'D RUN INTO YOU HERE.
HA HA HA
OH. IT'S NOT A COINCIDENCE.
WHAT?
YOU GUYS WERE TALKING SO LOUDLY ABOUT GOING TO THE BEACH...
THEN MIRAKO INVITED ME, SO I DECIDED TO COME.
HUH?
WHY DID YOU DO THAT?
I STARTED TO WONDER...
...HOW YOU'D REACT...
...WHEN YOU SAW THE OCEAN FOR THE FIRST TIME.
SHWAA
SHWAA

I LOVE THIS STORY!
WILL YOU READ ME THIS BOOK?
THAT ONE AGAIN?
THE SHELLS ARE ALL SO PRETTY!
SHWA A
HEY...
...WILL YOU TAKE ME TO THE OCEAN SOMEDAY?
The Story about the Ocean
I REMEMBER.
A LONG TIME AGO...
YOU REMEMBER...
...WHAT I SAID BACK THEN?

LET'S HEAD BACK.
AHH.
I'M ALWAYS...
...RECEIVING EVERYONE'S KINDNESS.
GRID

KIRA! GO AHEAD WITHOUT ME!
DASH
HIKARU?!
I WANT TO...
I THINK IT WAS OVER THERE.
THERE WERE LOTS.
...GIVE TOO.
EVEN IF KONPARU ENDS UP HATING ME...
...I WANT TO TELL HIM...
...HOW I FEEL.

GRAB
I THINK IT WAS OVER THERE...
ACK!
SHUMP
...
KONPARU...!

WHAT?
It's dangerous!
IDIOT!
S-SORRY!
WHAT IF YOU FELL IN LIKE YOU DID EARLIER?!
SHFF
WHAT ARE YOU DOING HERE ANYWAY?
IT'S...
...A TOKEN...
...OF THANKS...

THANK YOU FOR COMING TO THE OCEAN WITH ME TODAY.
IT MADE ME REALLY, REALLY...
...HAPPY.
SINCE I STARTED ATTENDING SHISHIKU...
...EVERY DAY HAS BEEN DAZZLING.
...ALL MY FRIENDS HAVE BEEN THERE FOR ME.
IT'S BECAUSE...
EVEN IF YOU DON'T LIKE ME ANYMORE...

...I'LL ALWAYS LIKE YOU!

YOU ALWAYS THINK ABOUT OTHERS FIRST.

YOU PUT ME AND THE OTHERS BEFORE YOURSELF...

DON'T HOLD BACK.
EVEN IF WE QUARREL, I'LL CONTINUE TO LIKE YOU.
WE'RE FRIENDS, RIGHT?
Y...
YEAH!

KON-PARU...
SO THAT'S WHAT YOU WANTED TO TELL ME.
ARE YOU CRYING?
N...
NO, MY EYES STILL STING FROM THE SEAWATER.
YOUR EYES WILL GET SWOLLEN IF YOU RUB THEM.
I'M HAPPY.
Urgh...
Don't move now.
THIS IS IT.
FRIEND-SHIP...

FRIEND-SHIP...?
GW
AR
TOTO-MARU!
...DOING OUT HERE TOGETHER ?!
...YOU...
...ARE...
WHAT...
TMP
TMP
TMP
TOMP
TOMP
TOMP

PO
IT
YOU ALWAYS ARGUE LIKE THAT.
THOP IT!
I WAS JUST WIPING HIS FACE.
LIAR!
IT DIDN'T LOOK THAT WAY.
THAT'S ALL IT WAS.
THEN WHY ARE YOU BLUSHING?! LOOK AT ME!
?!
SHUT UP, TOTOMARU.
I DON'T WANT TO SEE YOUR UGLY FACE.
YARI YARI
WHAT?! YOU WANNA FIGHT?
COME AT ME THEN.
Y...
YOU GUYS!
AH
I bit my tongue.
UH...
OKAY.

HEY...
...
IT'S THE FIRST TIME I'VE HAD FRIENDS.
YOU ALL WANT TO HANG OUT TONIGHT?
THERE ARE SO MANY THINGS...
...I DON'T KNOW.
THIS IS FOR YOU, KIRA.
?
Calm down, first-years.
HA HA HA
Woo! Cool!

I LOVE IT...
THE REAL OCEAN!
I'M LOOKING FORWARD TO LEARNING MORE.
FROM NOW ON...
...I WON'T BE ALONE...
KON-PARU!
OKAY.
FIREWORKS ARE LIT!
?

...BECAUSE I'VE GOT MY FRIENDS.
MY SUMMER...
...HAS JUST BEGUN.

Chapter
7

SEPTEMBER. SHISHIKU ACADEMY.
SUMMER VACATION IS OVER. IT'S BACK TO SCHOOL AS USUAL.
YOU'RE SO TANNED...
YOU LOOK LIKE COAL.
SHUT UP!
LOOK WHO'S TALKING!
GOT A PROBLEM?!
STRIP
SKUFF SKUFF
Go go go!
Bring it!
AH.
I'VE GOTTEN USED TO THIS.
EVERYONE'S SO FULL OF ENERGY.
FERVE
HEY, HIKARU.
YOU SOUND LIKE AN OLD MAN.
...don't faze me anymore.
Naked chests
I'M HINAKO NAKAYAMA.

THAT WAS CLOSE. I HAVE TO BE MORE CAREFUL.
AH HA HA HA
HIKARU, MY TWIN BROTHER, HATES THE ONIGASHIMA TRADITION OF HAVING TO BE BOSS OF SHISHIKU.
Yakuza are gross, smelly and bad!
BECAUSE I'M GOOD AT FIGHTING, WE SWITCHED PLACES FIVE MONTHS AGO.
OH.
THAT'S BECAUSE HIKARU SAID TO STOP TRYING TO BECOME THE BOSS OF SHISHIKU FOR NOW.
COME TO THINK OF IT, YOU HAVEN'T BEEN IN A FIGHT SINCE WE STARTED THE NEW TERM.
I MEANT THERE'S NO NEED TO RUSH THINGS!
HA HA HA HA HA
OH! NO!
OH
HIKARU?
YOU SEEM OUT OF IT. YOU OKAY?
AT FIRST I DIDN'T KNOW WHAT TO THINK OF THIS SCHOOL FOR DELINQUENTS.
BUT...
HEY, TOTOMARU!
B-BMP
ONE THING HAS BEEN BOTHERING ME LATELY...
BUT NOW I HAVE FRIENDS, AND I'M HAVING LOTS OF FUN.
YUP!

LOOK OUT! IT'S HIKARU ONIGASHIMA!
HA HA HA
KONPARU, DID YOU FINISH THE HOMEWORK FOR THE NEXT CLASS?
Can I copy it?
SWEET! THANKS!
HERE'S THE MAGAZINE I WAS TALKING ABOUT YESTERDAY!
JUST AS I THOUGHT.
OF COURSE I DIDN'T.
THERE'S DEFINITELY A DISTANCE BETWEEN ME AND EVERYONE ELSE!
...I DON'T EVEN KNOW HOW TO START UP A CONVERSATION.
BECAUSE I DIDN'T HAVE FRIENDS FOR SO LONG...
?
HIKARU...
YOU'RE RIGHT, BUT...
THEORY
AREN'T YOU OVERTHINKING IT?
JUST JUMP INTO A CONVERSATION.

HA HA
JUST KID-DING.
REALLY ?!
OKAY. I'LL HELP YOU OUT!
TEARY
...AREN'T WE ENOUGH ...?
THAT'S NOT WHAT I MEANT!
THANKS!
TOTO-MARU?
WHAT'S WRONG
GAAH!
I'M NOT GOING THROUGH THIS AGAIN!
HEEZE
HEEZE
HEEZE
HIKARU'S A GUY! WE'VE GOT THE SAME BODY PARTS!!
?
WELL, MY PROBLEMS ASIDE...

THERE'S A GREAT EVENT COMING UP WHERE YOU CAN MAKE FRIENDS!
WHAT IS IT?
SPORTS DAY WILL BE HELD NEXT WEEK!
YEAAH
IT'S THAT TIME OF THE YEAR AGAIN.
YOU GUYS READY?

WOW.
THEY'RE SO INTO IT!
AS YOU ALL KNOW, THE GRADES COMPETE AGAINST EACH OTHER AT OUR SCHOOL...
THIRD-YEARS, YOUR REPUTATION IS ON THE LINE. FIRST-YEARS AND SECOND-YEARS, TRY TO OVERTHROW YOUR UPPER-CLASSMEN. GOOD LUCK.
HOUOU IS THE JUDGE, SO HE WON'T PARTICIPATE IN THE GAMES.
SERIOUSLY, NO ONE HAS ANY HOPE AGAINST HIM.
WE LUCKED OUT THIS YEAR.
THERE'S NO POINT TELLING YOU NOT TO GET HURT, BUT...
...THIS HAPPENS ONLY ONCE A YEAR.
GO OUT AND MAKE IT AN EXPERIENCE YOU'LL NEVER FORGET!
HOUOU ...!
HE SAYS IT'S ONE GRADE AGAINST ANOTHER...
...BUT IN THE END, IT ALWAYS TURNS INTO A RIOT AND NOBODY KNOWS WHO'S WON OR LOST.
TMP

AH. YES! I PLAN TO.
HIKARU...
IT'LL BE DANGEROUS. ARE YOU TAKING PART?
KIRA, MIRAKO!
I'M GOING TO SKIP OUT AGAIN THIS YEAR.
I CAN'T STAND HOW SMELLY EVERYONE GETS.
I SEE...
THEN I WILL TOO.
MMM
SPORTS DAY, HUH?
Gotta train hard.
We'll win this one.
HEY, MIRAKO!
GET AWAY FROM HIKARU!
AAH
My suspicions are running wild.
I...
I'VE BEEN THINKING ABOUT IT, BUT YOU'RE RATHER ATTACHED TO THIS GUY, AREN'T YOU?
RINTARO! YOU'RE PARTICIPATING JUST BECAUSE OF HIKARU?
WHOA!
POKE
POKE

Now... Here's a mystery about Houou...

Apparently this has been bothering them for a long time.

Now it's starting to bother me too.

Maeno gives a straight answer.

Character designer Kinako Kuromitsu also came to the recording.

Something new has been established here.

BWA HA HA!
WHAT A JOKE.
LISTEN, EVERYONE!
I'M NERVOUS, BUT I'VE GOT TO DO MY BEST!
LET'S ALL WORK TOGETHER AS A TEAM!
HUH?
WHO'S THAT?! WHAT'S SO FUNNY?
!
THINK ABOUT IT.
YOU MAY TELL US TO CRUSH YEARS TWO AND THREE...
BUT HOW'S THAT GOING TO HAPPEN WHEN OUR BOSS IS SO TIGHT WITH THOSE UPPER-CLASSMEN?
ISN'T THAT RIGHT, HIKARU ONIGASHIMA?

SURE, TOTO-MARU, KON-PARU...
...KIRA AND MIRAKO ACCEPT YOU.
BUT DON'T THINK YOU GOT TO YOUR POSITION WITH THE ENTIRE GRADE BACKING YOU.
YOU CAN BE TOPPLED AT ANY TIME.
WHA-?
HEBIO! WAIT!
MUNEO HEBI-KAWA.
HE WAS NUMBER TWO AT HIYODORI MIDDLE SCHOOL, THE SAME SCHOOL KONPARU WENT TO.
THIS ISN'T GOOD...
MMMR
MMMR
HE'S RIGHT. OUR BOSS IS FRIENDLY WITH THE UPPER-CLASSMEN WE WANT TO BEAT...
WHAT JUST HAPPENED?
SUSPI-CIOUS...

TRUST ME!
I'LL DO ANYTHING FOR US TO WIN!
SO...
WHAT AM I GOING TO DO?
Damn, you're late!
Practice started already.
I HAVEN'T YET CONQUERED THE THIRD-YEARS...
...AND THIS TIME THE SECOND-YEARS ARE IN OUR SIGHTS.
But...
...Onigashima's the one who chose the time.
I want to go home already.
This sucks.
How long does this last?
WE WON'T WIN UNLESS OUR YEAR COMES TOGETHER.
YAWN

NOBODY'S FOCUSED, AND THERE'S NO TEAMWORK.
...
THIS IS BECAUSE I'M A WEAK LEADER!
HEY, I SEE YOU'RE WORKING HARD.
JMP
THAT'S NOT IT. I WANT US TO WIN ON SPORTS DAY TOO...
...SO I'VE BEEN THINKING ABOUT HOW WE CAN DO IT.
So here.
THIS IS FOR YOU.
Here's yours, Konparu.
SHOVE
HUH?
DON'T ACT SO BIG AND MIGHTY, YOU LAZY SON OF A B****!
YOU ...!

I THOUGHT YOU TWO LOOKING BRIGHT AND BEAUTIFUL WOULD HELP US GET A HIGH SCORE.
CHEERING IS ALSO AN IMPORTANT EVENT, RIGHT?
B
AM
WHAT?!!
SHISHIKU
I WANT YOU TO WEAR THEM. ♡
A cute salmon pink color...
BUT...
DRESSING LIKE A GIRL AGAIN?!
SHISHIKU
IF I'M NOT CAREFUL, THEY MIGHT FIND OUT I AM ONE!
DAMN YOU, HEBIO.
WHAT THE HELL?! WHY'D YOU DO THIS?!
YOU LOOKED CUTE DRESSED AS A GIRL AT MY CONCERT.
YOU MUST BE CRAZY!
THERE'S NO WAY I'D LOOK GOOD IN THIS!
That's right.
Yup. ♡
A wig too...
WHAP

TOTO-MARU...!
HIKARU IS OUR BOSS.
THERE'S NO WAY HE'S GONNA DRESS LIKE THAT.
YOU SAY THAT, BUT JUST IMAGINE...
GRRR
GURK
...ONIGASHIMA AS A CHEERLEADER. ♡
I GUARANTEE HE'LL LOOK CUTE...
SH-SHUT UP! IF YOU'RE THAT DESPERATE FOR SOMEONE TO DRESS LIKE A GIRL, I'LL DO IT!!
AARGH
YOU CAN'T, TOTO-MARU!!
WE'LL COME IN LAST FOR SURE.
GACK
Just stop!
PLIP
GRID
OKAY.

IF THIS WILL MAKE US WIN...
...I'LL DO IT!
JOLT
WHAT?
I CAN'T–
POFF
THEN WHY DON'T YOU CHANGE NOW?
WE HAVE TO MAKE SURE IT FITS.
HIKARU?!
I'LL DO IT IF IT MEANS I CAN REGAIN THEIR TRUST!
THEY'LL SEE MY BINDING.
WHAT? WHY NOT?
Hey!
STOP IT, HEBIO.
W-WAIT.
HMM...

HEY!!
BA
P
HOW LONG DO YOU PLAN TO HOG THE COURTYARD?
IT'S THE SECOND-YEARS' TURN NOW.
SKEE
GET OUT.

EXCUSE-
OUT OF MY WAY.
SHOVE
HIKARU!
KIRA!
DID YOU SEE THAT? SCARY...
THEY'RE NOT FRIENDLY.
WHAT?
...
KIRA...

I GET IT NOW.
PHOO
I'M GLAD.
I THINK...
...HE'S TRYING TO PROTECT YOU.
COOL
COLA
HE ACTED DISTANT BECAUSE HEBIO SAID YOU WERE TOO FRIENDLY WITH THE UPPER-CLASSMEN.
YOU'RE SO DUMB!
OH, OF COURSE!
WHAT? YOU THINK SO?
I THOUGHT HE IGNORED ME.
GRIT
WHEN DID YOU BECOME SO FRIENDLY?
...IS THERE SOMETHING BETWEEN YOU AND KIRA?
I'VE ALWAYS WON-DERED...

THAT'S NOT IT.
I'M THE ONE WHO HAS TO APOLOGIZE.
HUH?!
YOU NEVER TOLD ME!
Oh!
WE KNEW EACH OTHER WHEN WE WERE SMALL.
DIDN'T I TELL YOU?
Oh no!
SORRY THAT I FORGOT TO TELL YOU.
Is it that shocking?!
IT'S HOPELESS.
CRAP...
YET I KEEP WONDERING ABOUT YOUR RELATIONSHIP WITH KIRA.
...I CAN NEVER SEEM TO HELP YOU.
EVEN THOUGH I'M ALWAYS BY YOUR SIDE...
DON'T WORRY ABOUT IT!
IT'S REALLY NO BIG DEAL.
I SHOULD HAVE STOPPED THAT THING ABOUT DRESSING LIKE A GIRL...
TOTO-MARU...

I HATE...
...MYSELF.
LET'S WIN AND GET EVERYONE TO RECOGNIZE OUR YEAR!
SORRY ABOUT TODAY...
I'VE GOT YOUR BACK FROM NOW ON.

AS THE STRONGEST...
WHAT CAN I DO?
SOMEONE LIKE TOTOMARU SHOULD BE THE BOSS.
BECAUSE HE...
...WAS REALLY COOL JUST NOW.
B-BMP
B-BMP
Okay.
YOU NEED MUSCLE POWER TO BE THAT WAY.
I'VE GOT TO WORK ON THAT!
THE BRAIN MUSCLE !!
SWEAT
HUH?
THAT'S...
I NEVER THOUGHT HE'D AGREE TO WEAR A SKIRT.

TODAY'S HIKARU (REAL ONE)
This make-up is nice!
THAT'S NOT IT!!
I CAN'T REALLY ARGUE BECAUSE THAT IS WHAT HIKARU LIKES TO DO!
MAYBE THAT'S HIS SECRET HOBBY?
Oh man! Ha ha.
HE'S BECOME SUCH A WIMP.
I BET I CAN KNOCK HIM OUT WITH A SINGLE PUNCH.
ANYWAY, TOTOMARU CRACKS ME UP.
YANK
WHOA!
I WON'T LET...!
DROP IT.
IT'LL JUST MAKE YOUR REPUTATION WORSE.

THAT WAITER IS SO HAND-SOME...
HE'LL HEAR YOU!
TINK
KIRA?!
AAH...
HERE.
NO ONE HAS FOUND OUT BECAUSE SHISHIKU STUDENTS DON'T COME TO CAFÉS LIKE THIS.
YEAH.
KIRA... I DIDN'T KNOW YOU WERE WORKING PART-TIME HERE.
TOTOMARU WAS RIGHT.
HE'S THE SAME AS ALWAYS ...
THAT'S TRUE.

TINK
YES... BECAUSE I'M NOT A GOOD LEADER.
I HEARD FROM MIRAKO...
...THAT THE FIRST-YEARS ARE REBELLING.
B-BAD
BOW
THANK YOU FOR HELPING ME.
I SEEM TO ONLY CAUSE PROBLEMS FOR YOU AND TOTOMARU.
TOTOMARU, HUH?
YOU SEEM CLOSE TO HIM.
OH YES!
HE'S MY VERY FIRST FRIEND!

I SEE...
COOL.
SUFF
YOU CAN COUNT ON ME.
BUT...
...YOU TEND TO BE RECKLESS.
CAN YOU TAKE MY ORDER, WAITER?
I-
YES!
I'M LIKE A BIG BROTHER TO YOU, RIGHT?

BLUSH
ENJOY YOUR COFFEE.
TOTOMARU, HUH...
SO MANY PEOPLE HAVE SUP-PORTED ME.
THAT'S WHY I'M WHERE I AM TODAY.
Cafe
KA-CHAK
Thank you!

I WANT TO DO THE RIGHT THING...
...FOR EVERYONE.
I'M HIKARU ONIGASHIMA!
AS THE BOSS OF THE FIRST-YEARS, I'M GOING TO GIVE IT MY ALL!

Men Can Be Brave and Apologize!!

The three radio hosts apologize for the listeners who couldn't apologize. Each pretends to be a female listener.

In contrast to Aoi, who can maximize femininity and put on a perfect performance as a girl...

Maeno is pushing it, to be honest. (He has a deep voice.)

KENN found it so hilarious that he could barely speak.

It was like a crazy comedy act performed by three people. It was so funny to listen to. Please check out the CD of the radio program if you want to listen to the entire series. ✿

AND TODAY...

...IS SPORTS DAY.

...ARE YOU PUNKS READY? NOW...

LET'S RAISE HELL!

HAHAYE

GO, KON-PARU!
TOTOMARU BEAT FIVE PEOPLE ALL BY HIMSELF!
ONIGASHIMA IS SO FAST!
KIRA SET A NEW RECORD!
TOO FAST!

YO, HEBIO, AT THIS RATE...
Ha ha. DON'T PANIC.
I DIDN'T TAKE HIM SERIOUSLY AT FIRST...
...BUT ONIGASHIMA IS AMAZING!
Look this way!!
Young mis-tress!
Fighting spirit!
Good luck, young mis-tress!
NO WAY...
THOSE THREE WON ALL THE GAMES.
I'M GLAD THE GRUELING TRAINING PAID OFF!
1
HEEZE
HUFF
HEEZE
HE'LL BE EMBARRASSED AND CRY SOON.
THE TIME HAS COME.
FINALLY...

BA
HIKARU, KONPARU!
I'M FINE, TOTOMARU ...
I WON'T RUN AWAY AND LEAVE HIKARU ALONE.
SERIOUSLY, YOU DON'T HAVE TO DO THIS!
OKAY?
THAT'S RIGHT.
AT THIS POINT, WE JUST HAVE TO DO IT.
EVERYONE!
FWIP

WHOA
THE CHEER-LEADERS ARE HERE!
GIRLS! GIRLS HAVE DESCENDED ON SHISHIKU!
WHA–?!
H-HIKARU...!
HEE
COME ON, EVERYONE! YOU CAN DO IT! YOU CAN DO IT!
THERE'S ONLY ONE THING I CAN DO...
...BRING US VICTORY!
THAT GUY...
WHAT THE–?!
YARGH...
HE GOT TOUGHER MENTALLY TOO!
SPURT

...AND NOW HE'S CUTE TOO!
HE'S ALWAYS BEEN SO STRONG AND COOL...
FW
HOUOU IS LOSING IT!!
AM
WOW, THE FIRST-YEARS ARE THE OVER-WHELMING WINNER!
10
10
10000
WAAAAAH
...THE BEST!
THE BOSS OF OUR GRADE IS...
YOU GUYS! WHAT THE HELL?!
BESOTTED
HIKARU!!
HUFF
I CAN ALMOST SEE PANTIES.
HUFF
GO DIE!
FWAK
Phew!
THANKS, HIKARU'S SPIRIT...
I SOMEHOW DID IT!
ShiShiKu
GRR
...

HUH?
HURRY UP AND CHANGE ALREADY.
NO REASON!!
TOTO-MARU... WHY DO YOU KEEP LOOKING AWAY?
GOOD JOB.
YOU LOOKED LIKE SOME-ONE'S SISTER.
COOL MELON SODA
OUR GYM CLOTHES...!
HEY, YOU'VE GONE TOO FAR...
...EVEN IF WE WANT TO SEE HIKARU DRESSED AS A GIRL FOR A BIT LONGER.
OH, THOSE ... THEY WERE SO DIRTY, I THOUGHT THEY WERE TRASH.
SORRY, MAN.
HEBIO!!
SWAP

HAH?! WHAT'RE YOU TALKING ABOUT?
YOU GUYS ARE ALL GROSS.
AH!!
WHAT DID YOU JUST SAY?!
STOP IT!
Hey. THE NEXT GAME IS ABOUT TO START!
FWAAH
HIKARU.
Hey. HEBIO!
HERE... WRAP THIS AROUND YOU.

GLOW
THIS IS WHY I DIDN'T WANT YOU...
...TO DRESS LIKE THAT.
?
!
THANKS.
NEXT IS GRAB THE POLES!
THE TEAM THAT BRINGS BACK THE GREATEST NUMBER OF POLES...
...FROM THE MIDDLE OF THE FIELD TO THEIR BASE IS THE WINNER!
YOU'RE ALLOWED TO DO ANY-THING IT TAKES TO WIN!
THUD THUD THUD THUD THUD
YAARGH!
THRONG
?!

Get back, jerk!
TOTO-MARU, HELP–
FLUP
HIKARU!
SHUT UP! YOU'VE GOT SOME NERVE, FIRST-YEAR!
HEY! STOP TAKING ADVANTAGE OF THE SITUATION TO GET CLOSE TO OUR GODDESS!
WAIT! WHAT ABOUT THE POLES?
EEP!
PUSH
PUSH
PUSH
TOTO-MARU?!
POW
HEY! OVER THERE!
KIRA...

HEBIO!!
EEK...
THE THIRD-YEAR TEAM!
HE'S GOT NO HOPE.
LET'S JUST LEAVE HIM.
WE CAN'T GET TO HIM IN TIME.
Ah, shucks.
THEY'RE GOING TO BEAT HIM TO A PULP!
HIKARU?!
DASH
!!
AK

GET BACK.
YOU...
WHY WOULD YOU-
WHY?
THE BOSS ALWAYS PROTECTS HIS TEAM, RIGHT?

FIRST-YEARS WILL LOSE FAITH IN HIKARU IF I GO IN...
URGH!
OH?!
WE'RE NOT GOING TO GO EASY ON YOU JUST CUZ YOU'RE HOUOU'S LITTLE BROTHER!
THUK
AH!
GET THE HELL OVER THERE AND PROTECT HIM!
TOTO-MARU!
AREN'T YOU HIKARU'S FRIEND?

THU
ONIGA-
SHIMA
DAMN ...
THE
GRIT
SOR
I'M LA
HIKAR
TOTO-
MARU!
I'VE GOT
YOUR
BACK.

GYAAAA!
FWAM
FWAM
WHAT THE HECK?! LOOK AT THEM...
THEY MATCH EACH OTHER'S MOVES.
YEAH!!
WE'RE GONNA WIN!
THEY'RE SUPER-STRONG!
IN THE END...

...JUST AS KIRA PREDICTED...
...SPORTS DAY TURNED INTO A HUGE, FREE-FOR-ALL BRAWL.
GLO
YARGH !!
HEY, YOU THUGS...
HOUOU TOOK OUT EVERYONE WHO GOT TOO FEVERISH WITH EXCITEMENT.
Woo! Houou is the best!
HOUOU'S LEGENDARY STATUS BECAME EVEN GREATER, AND SPORTS DAY CAME TO AN END.
ENOUGH, I SAID.
OH.
OUCH.

VISH
GOOD-
Whoa!
SHFF
HEBIO!!
...
I HATE IT.
HE STILL DOESN'T ACCEPT ME AS THE BOSS?!
WHAT?!
SHFF
Medicin
Works wel
injuries
IF YOU OWE SOMEONE, IT FEELS LIKE THAT PERSON HAS THE DIRT ON YOU, RIGHT?
HERE. LET'S CALL IT EVEN.

YOU CAN DO THAT, RIGHT?
AFTER ALL, YOU'RE THE BOSS OF OUR YEAR.
HEBIO...
YOU FINALLY GET IT?
SPORTS DAY IS OVER ALREADY.
TAKE IT EASY, TOTOMARU!
HEY! HEBIO'S BEING SNEAKY!
WHOA!
DON'T BE SELFISH!
HE'S OUR BOSS TOO!
FWIP
POK
GAK

AAH...
FINALLY...
...I'VE BECOME FRIENDS WITH THEM ALL.
Sorry! Sorry!
KRIK KRIK KRIK
Go, Konparu!
FEAVER
YEAH. SPORTS DAY IS OVER...
...BUT I'LL NEVER FORGIVE YOU, HEBIO...
URK!!
TOTO-MARU.
YEAH?
THANKS FOR COMING TO MY RESCUE YESTERDAY.
YOU'RE THE GREATEST BEST FRIEND I COULD EVER ASK FOR!

OF COURSE I AM!
Get him, Konpaku!
I give up! I give up! I give up!
Ah. KIRA!
OH
SOUNDS LIKE EVERY-ONE'S HAVING FUN.
UM. YES!
I THINK EVERY-THING'S OKAY NOW.
GRAAH
TUG
UM...
THANKS FOR WORRYING ABOUT ME...
..."BIG BROTHER!"

SMILE
HIKA-
ME TOO.
THANKS.
DON'T WORRY ANYMORE, KIRA. HE'S GOT ME AS HIS BEST FRIEND!
RIGHT.
BUT IT'S A BIG BURDEN.
I CAN ALWAYS TAKE OVER IF IT GETS TO BE TOO MUCH FOR YOU.
AHHH...
SUFF
?

"BIG BROTHER," HUH...
WHY DO I STILL FEEL THIS WAY WHEN HINAKO'S SAFE?
I SHOULD BE HAPPY TO BE CALLED HIS BEST FRIEND.
WHY DO I FEEL SO CONFUSED?
I DON'T KNOW WHAT'S GOING ON, BUT ONE THING I KNOW FOR SURE...
...IS THAT I DON'T WANT TO LOSE TO THIS GUY!!
SPORTS DAY WAS SO MUCH FUN!
PLAY A GAME

Chapter
8

IT'S STILL COLD OUTSIDE. IT'S FEBRUARY.
IT'S CUTER THIS WAY.
HIKARU ...
...YOU'LL CATCH COLD WITH BARE LEGS.
BRR!
YOUNG MISTRESS! YOU FORGOT THIS!
OOPS.
I'M HINAKO NAKA-YAMA.
AND THIS IS MY TWIN BROTHER, HIKARU ONIGA-SHIMA.
WE GO ABOUT OUR DAILY LIVES EVEN THOUGH WE'VE SWITCHED PLACES.
THANKS, SAKAGUCHI.

THE ONIGASHIMA FAMILY IS PART OF THE YAKUZA, BUT HIKARU LOATHES FIGHTING.
I'M GOING ON AHEAD.
Get off me, you pervert!
YOUNG BOSS... PLEASE DON'T HATE ME!
YOUNG BOSS!
HUFF
SAKAGUCHI! PUT THAT AWAY!
HUFF
YOU'LL GET MOLESTED IF YOU EXPOSE YOUR BEAUTIFUL LEGS LIKE THAT!
THIS IS WHAT I HATE ABOUT YOU!
I'LL ESCORT YOU TO SCHOOL.
I GREW UP IN AN ORPHANAGE, AND THE ONLY THING I'M GOOD AT IS FIGHTING.
I ENDED UP AT THE SCHOOL FOR DELINQUENTS IN HIKARU'S PLACE.
SKFF
THIS IS THE SCHOOL.
HEY, HIKARU.
SHISHIKU ACADEMY.
GOOD MORNING!
Yo.
HIKARU!

MIRAKO ...
DID YOU COME TO SCHOOL STRAIGHT FROM A PHOTO SHOOT AGAIN?
YES.
THINGS ARE GOING REALLY WELL.
YOU WANT TO BE AN IDOL TOO?
I THINK YOU'D BE POPULAR.
REALLY?
GACK!!
STOP IT!!
BWP
T...
TOTO-MARU...
I CAN'T... BREATHE.
URK URK URK
SQUEEZE
MIRAKO !!
DON'T GET COZY WITH HIKARU.
Oh? THERE'S TOTO, THE LOYAL DOG.
YANK

Ha ha. He took him away.
WHAT?!
KIRA...
YOU OKAY?
WE'LL BE TARDY!
LET'S GO, HIKARU!
YEAH!
GASP
DONG DONG
KIRA!
SCHOOL IS CRAZY...
EVEN WHEN I BECOME A SECOND-YEAR...
...BUT SO MUCH FUN.
...I WANT TO KEEP ENJOYING SCHOOL WITH THESE GUYS.

WELL...
THAT'S WHAT I HOPED...
IF I DON'T PASS THE MAKEUP EXAM, I HAVE TO REPEAT YEAR ONE...
I SUD-DENLY... GOT CALLED IN.
AN AMBUSH?! WHO DID THIS?!
KONPARU ?! WHAT'S WRONG?!
HIKARU. TOTO-MARU.
UGH...
Shishiku Academy Annual Report Card
FLUT
Grade 1, will be repeated with more than five 1s.
WHAAAAT ?!
WE HAVE A HUGE PROBLEM ON OUR HANDS.
I TOLD YOU THAT'S WRONG!
YOU HAVE TO FIRST MULTIPLY THE NUMBERS OUTSIDE THE PARENTHE-SES!
On the fast

While drawing *Bancho*...

I thought about this seriously. As a result...

The best way is to get Sakaguchi to somehow attend too so he can protect me!

STRONGEST!!

What do you think? What? Would that be against the rules? I see... It made me realize how amazing Hinako is because she's just as strong as all the delinquents (if not stronger). If I were to use my fist to fight, I'd break bones. The ones in my hands, that is.

GROUP TO AVOID FAILING AT ALL COSTS

IS THIS A SORT OF CODE?

DIDN'T YOU LEARN THIS IN GRADE SCHOOL?

Math I

Stay calm and try again.

SEETHE

?

?!

AAH

FLR

!

HEY...

TOTOMARU, YOU'RE SURPRISINGLY SMART.

WHAT DO YOU MEAN BY SURPRISINGLY?

WHAT ARE YOU STARING AT?
TOTO-MARU...
LOOK AT KON-PARU.
WHAT ARE YOU DOING, YOU IDIOT?!
HEH HEH
Burn...
ONE THING...
Aagh!
What the heck does X and Y mean anyway?!
No!! Don't think like that.
...AFTER ANOTHER.
BLEARY
FOR NOW...
...I'LL AIM FOR 40 POINTS.

This is the last sidebar. All the characters in "Love's Battle Royale" are wild yet compassionate, so I enjoyed drawing them. I hope I'll be able to draw them again soon...

There's a lot more in the works—an anime and more manga—and I'd be really happy if you'll continue to enjoy the world of *Kenka Bancho Otome*.

To my editor
Everyone at RED
Everyone at Spike
Chunsoft
All the voice actors
Anzai
Gondahara
My publisher
And every single reader

Thank you very much!!

FERVENT
LET'S PROMISE THAT WE ALL...
...WILL BECOME SECOND-YEARS TOGETHER!
AS LONG AS YOU'RE WITH FRIENDS...
...THE EVENTS IN EACH SEASON...
I DIDN'T KNOW BEFORE BECAUSE I WAS ALWAYS ALONE.
YEAH!
...AND THE USUAL ROUTE HOME...
EVERYTHING BECOMES SPECIAL.
THAT'S...
SHUT UP AND HAND OVER YOUR MONEY!
WHAT DID YOU SAY?!
OH
I HOPE WE'LL ALL BE IN THE SAME CLASS...

STOP IT, GUYS!
GO! RUN!
!
HEY! THAT'S SHISHIKU'S ONIGA-SHIMA!
What?!
WHO THE HELL CARES.
TAKE THAT!
THEY'RE WEAK...
ONE PUNCH SHOULD DO IT.
HIKARU!
GET BACK!!
SHIK
OH!

FERV
A KNIFE?!
T...
TOTOMARU!!
ITO HOSPITAL
OW, OW, OW! CAN'T YOU BE MORE GENTLE?!

WHAT?!
YOU'RE ALL SET.
SOMEONE FROM YOUR FAMILY IS HERE.
IT WAS MY FAULT FOR NOT BEING MORE AWARE.
THOSE DIRTY JERKS...
THEY RAN OFF FAST.
WHY DID YOU CALL THEM WITHOUT ASKING ME FIRST?!
SHOCK
HIDE, HIKARU!
WHAT'S THE MATTER, TOTO-
TOTO-MARU!
BAM

DAD...
OH...
TOTO-MARU'S FATHER.
THEY SEEM SO DIFFERENT.
HIKARU, LEAVE NOW.
BUT I SHOULD AT LEAST SAY HELLO.
OH!
DON'T PULL ON THE WOUND!
OW!
GLARE
SO YOU'RE THE FAMOUS HIKARU ONIGA-SHIMA...
I WANT YOU TO HAVE NOTHING TO DO WITH MY SON.
NOT THAT IT MAT-TERS...
YOU WON'T SEE HIM AGAIN BECAUSE HE'S GOING TO QUIT SHISHIKU.

WHAT'RE YOU TALKING ABOUT?!
WHAT?
IDIOT!
A PROMISE IS A PROMISE.
THIS WAS JUST AN ACCIDENT.
OW! OW! OW!
B-
IF YOU CAN'T KEEP A SIMPLE PROMISE, YOU HAVE NO RIGHT TO COMPLAIN.
HIKARU ...!
TOTOMARU!
DON'T WORRY ABOUT ME.
SEE YOU AT SCHOOL TOMORROW.
BMP
SLAM
TOTOMA-

WHAT'S GOING ON?!
SINE, COSINE, TANGENT...
PRIVATE LAND OWNER-SHIP LAW...
AH...
TOTO-MARU MISSED SCHOOL AGAIN TODAY.
IDIOTS NEVER GET SICK, SO THIS ISN'T LIKE HIM AT ALL.
TIME FOR YOUR TEST, KONPARU! GOOD LUCK!!
I GOT THIS ONE.
I'M NOT DUMB ANY-MORE...
YEAH...

YOU'RE ALONE...
THAT'S RARE.
OH
Totomaru
Sorry. Not going to school today.
Because of yesterday?
Sort of.
Don't worry! Just make sure Konparu doesn't slack off.
Got it!
Today
Not going in today.
Are you okay? Do you need to talk?
Everyone's worried.
Konparu is about to
KIRA.
YEAH...
KONPARU IS TAKING HIS MAKEUP TEST. AND TOTOMARU IS ABSENT TODAY.
I FEEL KIND OF LOST.

I WONDER WHY.
I SHOULD BE USED TO BEING ALONE...
...BUT I'M WOR-RIED.
I'M WOR-RIED ABOUT KON-PARU'S TEST...
...AND HOW TOTOMARU IS DOING RIGHT NOW.
I KEEP THINKING ABOUT THINGS LIKE THAT...
IT'S A GOOD THING.
HUH?
IT MEANS YOU'VE MADE GOOD FRIENDS.

DON'T WORRY TOO MUCH.
TRUST THEM.
THOSE TWO...
YES!
HE'S RIGHT.
THEY'RE GOING TO BE ALL RIGHT.
YOU KNOW WHAT TOTOMARU AND KONPARU ARE LIKE, RIGHT?
THIS PAST YEAR...
...WE OVER-CAME SO MANY OBSTACLES TOGETHER.

I'M SURE THIS TIME...
...THEY'LL SUCCEED TOO.
THAT'S WHY...
FLIP
HEH
I DON'T HAVE TO STUDY ANYMORE!
JEEZ, KONPARU...
KLAK
THANK YOU.
OH.
TOTOMARU!
JOLT
FERVENT

HEY, TOTO-MARU!
I'VE CLEARED MY NAME.
THE MAKEUP TEST WENT WELL. SO WE CAN ALL MOVE UP TOGETHER.
HIKARU...
I'M SO HAPPY! YOU'RE BACK AT SCHOOL!
THAT'S NOT GOING TO HAPPEN. SORRY.
I'M QUITTING SHISHIKU...
...TO GO STUDY ABROAD.
HUH?

I'M LEAVING AT THE WEEKEND, SO I'M BUSY GETTING READY.
SEE YOU GUYS LATER.
I'M SERI-OUS.
YOU'RE JOKING, RIGHT?
WHY SUD-DENLY...
WHAT?!
WAIT!
I SORT OF KNEW FROM BEFORE THAT STAYING AT SHISHIKU...
...WOULDN'T BE GOOD FOR MY FUTURE.
Oh...
MY DAD HAS NOTHING TO DO WITH THIS.
LOOK AT ME WHEN YOU TALK!
VUP
DID SOME-THING HAPPEN BETWEEN YOU AND YOUR DAD?!
WE SAID WE'D BECOME SECOND-YEARS TOGETHER.

FERVENT
GET LOST!
DON'T BOTHER ME ANYMORE.
T-
WHAT...?
JUST BECAUSE YOU'RE SMART DOESN'T MEAN-
DON'T GET CARRIED AWAY, YOU DUMB IDIOT.
Ha!
I DON'T WANT A GUY WHO FLUNKS TO LECTURE ME.
HEY.
THAT'S NO WAY TO TALK.
HIKARU HAS BEEN WORRIED ABOUT YOU THIS WHOLE TIME.
YOU-
STOP IT!

TOTOMARU!!
DASH
...
FEVER
WE'RE FRIENDS!
I DON'T WANT TO SEE YOU TWO FIGHT.

I'M RELIEVED.
YOU'LL BE IN A GOOD ENVIRONMENT FOR STUDYING AT THE NEW SCHOOL.
IT'S NIGHT AND DAY COMPARED TO THIS DUMP.
VROOM
OF COURSE.
UNLIKE SOMEONE WHO BROKE IT FIRST.
YOU MADE A PROMISE TO ME.
YOU'RE GOING TO KEEP IT, RIGHT?
KLENCH
WHY DIDN'T HE SAY SOMETHING TO US FIRST?
HE'S LEAVING THIS WEEKEND.
THAT'S ONLY TWO DAYS FROM NOW.

I GUESS HE DOESN'T CARE ABOUT US...
DON'T WORRY TOO MUCH...
TRUST THEM.
THAT'S NOT TRUE...
THERE'S NO WAY TOTOMARU DOESN'T CARE ABOUT US!
!
FERVEN
THE TOTOMARU I KNOW...
...IS THAT KIND OF GUY.
...AND IS ALWAYS GOOD TO HIS FRIENDS.
HE LOVES SHISHIKU...

THERE'S GOT TO BE A GOOD REASON.
LET'S LOOK INTO IT AND FIND OUT!
HIKARU...
...DID SOMETHING HAPPEN BETWEEN HIM AND HIS DAD?
YEAH...
THEY SAID SOMETHING ABOUT A PROMISE.
I SEE.
YES!
TOTO-MARU...
...MIGHT THINK WE'RE BEING ANNOYING...
DASH

LET ME HELP TOO.
...BUT I...
...WANT TO BELIEVE IN...
...MY BEST FRIEND TOTOMARU.
TOTOMARU'S FAMILY VALUES EDUCATION...
...AND HE'S ALWAYS DONE WELL AT SCHOOL SINCE HE WAS A LITTLE KID.

BIP
BUT IN THE WINTER OF HIS THIRD YEAR IN MIDDLE SCHOOL ...
...HE GOT CAUGHT UP IN A FRIEND'S FIGHT, AND HIS PLACE AT A TOP HIGH SCHOOL WAS RESCINDED.
ONLY SHISHIKU WOULD ACCEPT HIM, BUT HIS DAD WAS OPPOSED TO HIM ATTENDING.
THIS VIDEO IS FROM THE OTHER DAY.
IT'S FOOTAGE FROM THE SECURITY CAMERA AT THE CONVENIENCE STORE.
IT LOOKS LIKE YOUNG BOSS ATTACKED FIRST.
TOTOMARU'S DAD GOT AHOLD OF THIS AND SAID...
..."QUIT SHISHIKU IF YOU DON'T WANT ME TO SUE HIKARU ONIGASHIMA FOR GETTING YOU INVOLVED IN THIS."
THAT'S THE BARGAIN HE PROPOSED.
!
THAT'S NOT WHAT HAPPENED!
WE WERE TRYING TO HELP SOMEONE WHO WAS BEING MUGGED.
TOTOMARU TRIED TO TELL HIS DAD THAT.
AS LONG AS THE STUDENT FROM THE OTHER SCHOOL DOESN'T COME FORWARD...
...HIS DAD WON'T LISTEN TO SHISHIKU KIDS LIKE US.

TOTOMARU IS LEAVING HOME TODAY TO CATCH TOMORROW'S FLIGHT...
...HE HAS A RESERVATION FOR THE BULLET TRAIN AT 5 PM.
WHAT?
THAT'S SOON!
WE'VE GOT TO HURRY!
HIKARU.
WE'VE GOT TO TALK HIS DAD OUT OF IT, OTHERWISE THE PROBLEM WON'T BE RESOLVED.
WE NEED TO DO MORE THAN JUST STOP TOTOMARU!
HOW DO WE DO THAT?
!
FLAK
BAM
IS IT TRUE TOTOMARU IS BEING SENT TO ANOTHER COUNTRY?!
HIKARU, WE WANT TO HELP TOO!
GUYS...!

HIKARU! LEAVE IT UP TO US TO CONVINCE HIS DAD.
I HAVE AN IDEA.
OH
CALM DOWN, GUYS.
IDIOT! WE SHOULD JUST KIDNAP HIS DAD.
THE BEST WAY IS TO HIJACK THE PLANE!
GRAAH
GRAAH
I CAN'T HEAR WHAT EVERYONE'S SAYING...
KON-PARU...
YOU'RE THE ONLY ONE WHO CAN STOP TOTOMARU.
I'M COUNTING ON YOU.
MIRAKO!
I'M HEADING TO A PHOTO SHOOT...
...AND IT'S NEAR THE STATION.
HEY, HEY... WHAT'S GOING ON?
WE NEED TO GET READY. CAN WE BORROW SAKA-GUCHI'S CAR?
BUT THE STATION IS IN THE OPPOSITE DIREC-TION...
IT'S TOO FAR WITHOUT A CAR.
TMP

LEAVE THE REST TO KONPARU AND THE OTHERS.
LET'S GO, HIKARU.
OKAY!
KLENCH
THAT IDIOT.
LET'S GO!
YEAH!!
HIKARU NEEDS...
...BOTH OF US.

...
VROOM
SHH.
IT'S A PROBLEM.
YOU'LL BE LATE FOR SURE IF WE GO BY THE STATION FIRST...
UM... IF YOU'RE LATE, YOU CAN JUST DROP US OFF SOMEWHERE.
SHALL WE GO STRAIGHT TO THE SHOOT?
FORGET ABOUT THAT OTHER GUY.
YOU CAN WATCH ME SHOW OFF INSTEAD.
OH, UM...
!
YOU KNOW THAT MOVIE I REFUSED TO DO?
YOU CAN TELL THE DIRECTOR I'D LOVE TO ACCEPT THE ROLE.

STOP IT, MIRAKO.
YOU'RE MAKING IT HARDER ON HIKARU.
HA HA HA
OKAY, OKAY.
YOU'RE SO BORING, RINTARO.
HE'S SO ADORABLE. I LOVE TEASING HIM!
SKREEK
HERE'S THE STATION!
SO...
...MAKE SURE YOU HOLD ON TO THAT GUY'S LEASH AND DON'T LET GO.
THANK YOU!
MIRAKO...

THERE HE IS!
HUFF
HUFF
T...
GET LOST!
OH
...

TUP
KIRA?
I'LL ALWAYS ...
...REGRET THAT I LEFT YOU ALL THOSE YEARS AGO.
I DON'T WANT YOU...
...TO FEEL THAT WAY TOO.
USE YOUR FISTS...
...TO BRING HIM BACK...
...HINAKO.

TOTO-MARU!!
KIRA...
GRIT
DASH
2
777
a great vic
in the life

HIKARU?!
WHAT THE-?!
YWP
I'M NOT MOVING.
LEAVE.
I TOLD YOU NOT TO BOTHER ME ANYMORE.
YOU CAN PRETEND TO BE MEAN, BUT IT WON'T WORK.
...
YOUR DAD...
...THREATENED TO SUE ME...
...THAT'S WHY YOU'RE GOING ABROAD, RIGHT?
!

YOU'RE WRONG...
YEAH...
KLENCH
IT'S GOT NOTHING TO DO WITH YOU, HIKARU!
OKAY THEN.
IF YOU WANT TO GET PAST ME, YOU HAVE TO KNOCK ME DOWN FIRST!
I'M LEAVING SHISHIKU BECAUSE I WANT TO!
WHAT...?
CAN YOU DO IT, TOTO-MARU?
I'M THE STRONGEST OF YEARS ONE AND TWO.
I'VE...

...ALWAYS BEEN AT YOUR SIDE...
...SO YOU SHOULD KNOW!
THAT'S WHY...
COME ON!
...I DON'T WANT...
HIKARU...
WHAT'RE YOU SAYING?

HOW DO YOU PLAN TO FIGHT ME...WITH THOSE FISTS?
...TO BE SEPARATED...
...FROM YOU.
!
VHRRR VHRRR
B
I CAME TO APOLO-GIZE!
I'M SO SORRY!
I'M THE ONE IN THE VIDEO!
NO, IT'S ME!
I AM
DAD?! WHAT?
TOTO-MARU?! WHAT'S THIS ALL ABOUT?!

EVERYONE IS ME?
HUH?!
WHAT?!
IT'S RIGHT HERE IN THE VIDEO.
EVEN IF YOU SMASH UP THIS ONE, I MADE OTHER COPIES!
HIKARU ONIGASHIMA IS NOT HERE!
THIS IS KONPARU'S PLAN?
WHO ARE YOU GUYS?!
URGH...
...HIKARU ONIGASHIMA REALLY IS A DELINQUENT!!
WHAT A HALF-BAKED IDEA...
THUD
I SEE.
LET'S SETTLE THIS ONCE AND FOR ALL.

HOUOU!!
THESE TWO PUNKS ARE THE REAL CULPRITS.
WE'RE SORRY!
WE'RE THE ONES WHO STARTED THE FIGHT.
YANK
YO, HIKARU.
ACK!
WELL...
I WAS PLANNING TO KEEP A LOW PROFILE UNTIL GRADUATION.
AH...
DAD...
BUT I HAD TO COME TO MY DEAR LITTLE BROTHER'S DEFENSE.

HURRY UP AND COME BACK, TOTO-MARU.
AREN'T WE ALL BECOMING SECOND-YEARS TOGETHER?
...
I KEPT MY PART OF THE BARGAIN. WHAT ABOUT YOU?
KONPARU–
PRO
UD
THESE SCORES ARE PATHETIC, IDIOT!
HEY, YOU BARELY PASSED!
31
30
32
KON-PARU...
You seemed so confident after the test...
AH, CRAP.
THIS IS DRIVING ME CRAZY.
FLUMP
...
DAD.

PLEASE LET ME STAY AT SHISHIKU.
...AND I WON'T CAUSE ANY PROBLEMS FOR YOU.
THIS TIME FOR SURE I'LL KEEP MY PROMISE TO STAY OUT OF TROUBLE...
...AND EVERY-ONE...
BUT SHISHIKU...
IT'S TRUE THEY'RE ALL DUMB...
...AND HIKARU... I LOVE THEM ALL!

SIGH
YOU HAVEN'T CHANGED ONE BIT, SON.
FINE.
HUH?
YOU HAVE TO PROMISE ONE MORE THING.
NEVER, EVER...
...GET HURT OR PUT YOURSELF IN DANGER.
DOES THAT MEAN...?
TOTO-MARU!
WHOA!
STOP-
GLOMP
I'm so happy!

SUFF
I DON'T THINK I'LL EVER...
...BE BETTER THAN YOU.
NOW...
...IT'S SPRING.

NOW THAT HOUOU GRADUATED...
...YOU'RE THE BOSS OF THE SCHOOL, HIKARU.
LET'S GO! LET'S SHOW THE NEWBIES HOW STRONG-
OH NO...
THE WIND IS BLOWING HOUOU'S JACKET AWAY!
HOW DID HE ALWAYS KEEP HIS JACKET ON?
FORTITUDE!
YOU...!
SHUFF
DON'T UNDRESS HERE!
SO LOUD...
YOU'RE BOTH SECOND-YEARS NOW, BUT YOU'RE STILL LIKE YAPPY PUPPIES.
THIS ISN'T MY STYLE.
I'M GOING TO WEAR WHAT I ALWAYS DO.
HIKARU...

TAKE IT EASY. JUST KEEP DOING WHAT YOU ALWAYS DO.
BEING TRUE TO WHO YOU ARE...
...IS WHAT WE EXPECT FROM THE BOSS.
KIRA...
HOLD ON!
IT'S MY JOB AS HIS FIRST BEST FRIEND AND HIS RIGHT-HAND MAN TO SAY THAT KIND OF THING!
THIRD-YEARS SHOULD CONCENTRATE ON STUDYING FOR COLLEGE ENTRANCE EXAMS!
BUT I'M THE ONE WHO HELPED HIKARU WHEN SOMEONE PULLED A SELFISH DISAPPEARING ACT.
ARGH...
STING
Hikaru
Good luck with the new term.♡
Now that you're a second-year, show the first-years who's in charge!
Hurry up and win! Promise!
HIKARU...
...IS RELENTLESS...
...LIKE ALWAYS, I GUESS.
SLAM
YAAH!

LET'S GO, HIKARU!
BAM
I'M GOING TO BE BOSS OF SHISHIKU, HIKARU ONIGA-SHIMA!
CRAZY...
...BUT FUN AND SPECIAL TIMES...
READY!
...UNDER THE FLAG OF SHISHIKU.
IT'S THE START OF ANOTHER DAY.
WHAT MESSAGE CAN WE SEND WITH OUR FISTS TODAY?
Vol. 2/End

A SCRAPBOOK THAT MAKES THE HEART FLUTTER

GOT IN LINE AFTER CHANGING WIGS THREE TIMES

In the Japanese version, there was a typo. Instead of "Kenka Bancho Otome," there was "Kenka Bancho Oyome." *Oyome* as in "bride"... Sounds very tough. Here is volume 2! Thank you for reading it!

—CHIE SHIMADA

Chie Shimada's first graphic novel *Renai Democlassic* released in 2011. Her other titles include *Sakura Taisen Kanadegumi* and *Nonnoma* (Drink Responsibly!) She loves drinking and cats.

Kenka Bancho Otome: Love's Battle Royale Vol. 2

SHOJO BEAT MANGA EDITION

STORY AND ART BY
Chie Shimada

ORIGINAL CONCEPT BY
Spike Chunsoft

VIDEO GAME DEVELOPED BY
Red Entertainment

TRANSLATION **JN Productions**
TOUCH-UP ART & LETTERING **Inori Fukuda Trant**
GRAPHIC DESIGN **Alice Lewis**
EDITOR **Nancy Thistlethwaite**

KENKABANCHO OTOME -KOI NO BATTLE ROYALE-
by CHIE SHIMADA / SPIKE CHUNSOFT / RED ENTERTAINMENT
© Chie Shimada 2017
© Spike Chunsoft Co., Ltd. All Rights Reserved. Developed by RED.
All rights reserved.
First published in Japan in 2017 by HAKUSENSHA, Inc., Tokyo.
English language translation rights arranged with HAKUSENSHA, Inc., Tokyo.

The stories, characters and incidents mentioned in this publication are entirely fictional.

No portion of this book may be reproduced or transmitted in any form or by any means without written permission from the copyright holders.

Printed in Canada

Published by VIZ Media, LLC
P.O. Box 77010
San Francisco, CA 94107

10 9 8 7 6 5 4 3 2 1
First printing, July 2018

viz.com

shojobeat.com

Now available in a 2-in-1 edition!

Maid-sama!

As if being student council president of a predominantly male high school isn't hard enough, Misaki Ayuzawa has a major secret—she works at a maid café after school! How is she supposed to keep her image of being ultrasmart, strong and overachieving intact once school heartthrob Takumi Usui discovers her double life?!

Shojo Beat

viz media
www.viz.com

Kaicho wa Maid Sama! © Hiro Fujiwara 2006/HAKUSENSHA, Inc.

Can she clean up her act...

...and STILL kick some butt?

ORESAMA TEACHER

Izumi Tsubaki

Story & art by Izumi Tsubaki

Determined to make the best of the situation and make her mother proud, Mafuyu decides to turn over a new, feminine, well-behaved leaf. But her fighting spirit can't be kept down, and the night before school starts she finds herself defending some guy who's getting beaten up. One slip wouldn't have been a problem, except the guy is ***...her teacher?!*** How can Mafuyu learn to be a good girl if her teacher won't let her forget her wicked past?

Oresama Teacher, Vol. 1
ISBN: 978-1-4215-3863-1 • $9.99 US / $12.99 CAN

IN STORES NOW!

www.viz.com

ORESAMA TEACHER © Izumi Tsubaki 2008/HAKUSENSHA, Inc.

FROM THE CREATOR OF VAMPIRE KNIGHT

Shuriken and Pleats

When the master she has sworn to protect is killed, Mikage Kirio, a skilled ninja, travels to Japan to start a new, peaceful life for herself. But as soon as she arrives, she finds herself fighting to protect the life of Mahito Wakashimatsu, a man who is under attack by a band of ninja. From that time on, Mikage is drawn deeper into the machinations of his powerful family.

www.viz.com

Shuriken to Pleats © Matsuri Hino 2015/HAKUSENSHA, Inc.

IDOL dreams

STORY & ART BY
ARINA TANEMURA

At age 31, office worker Chikage Deguchi feels she missed her chances at love and success. When word gets out that she's a virgin, Chikage is humiliated and wishes she could turn back time to when she was still young and popular. She takes an experimental drug that changes her appearance back to when she was 15. Now Chikage is determined to pursue everything she missed out on all those years ago—including becoming a star!

www.viz.com

Thirty One idream © Arina Tanemura 2014/HAKUSENSHA, Inc.

yoko Mogami followed her true love Sho to Tokyo to support him while he made it big as an idol.
t he's casting her out now that he's famous enough! Kyoko won't suffer in silence–
e's going to get her sweet revenge by beating Sho in show biz!

Vol. 1 ISBN: 978-1-4215-4226-3
Vol. 2 ISBN: 978-1-4215-4227-0
Vol. 3 ISBN: 978-1-4215-4228-7

Show biz is sweet...but revenge is sweeter!

In Stores Now!

Skip·Beat!

Story and Art by YOSHIKI NAKAMURA

Skip•Beat! © Yoshiki Nakamura 2002/HAKUSENSHA, Inc.

A **Publisher's Weekly** bestseller!

What happens when the hottest boy in school
...is a girl?!

Find out in these 3-in-1
collections of the hit shojo series

Hana-Kimi

Story & Art by HISAYA NAKAJO

Mizuki Ashiya has such a crush on a track star named Izumi Sano that she moves from the U.S. to Japan to enroll in the all-male high school he goes to! Pretending to be a boy, Mizuki becomes Sano's roommate...

...but how can she keep such a big secret when she's so close to the guy she wants?

IN STORES NOW!

3-in-1 Vol. 1 ISBN: 978-1-4215-4224-9
3-in-1 Vol. 2 ISBN: 978-1-4215-4225-6
3-in-1 Vol. 3 ISBN: 978-1-4215-4229-4

Only **$14.99 US / $16.99 CAN** each!

www.viz.com

Hanazakari no Kimitachi he
© Hisaya Nakajo 1996/HAKUSENSHA, Inc.

STOP!

You may be reading the wrong way!

In keeping with the original Japanese comic format, this book reads from right to left—so action, sound effects and word balloons are completely reversed to preserve the orientation of the original artwork.

Check out the diagram shown here to get the hang of things, and then turn to the other side of the book to get started!

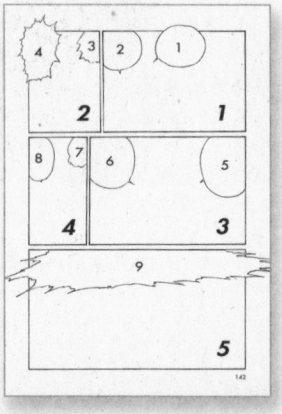